HEALTHY FRIENDSHIPS

By Emma Huddleston

CONTENT CONSULTANT

Dr. Amanda J. Rose
Professor of Psychological Sciences
University of Missouri

Essential Library

An Imprint of Abdo Publishing | abdobooks.com

abdobooks.com

Published by Abdo Publishing, a division of ABDO, PO Box 398166, Minneapolis, Minnesota 55439. Copyright © 2021 by Abdo Consulting Group, Inc. International copyrights reserved in all countries. No part of this book may be reproduced in any form without written permission from the publisher. Essential Library™ is a trademark and logo of Abdo Publishing.

Printed in the United States of America, North Mankato, Minnesota.
082020
012021

Cover Photo: Gpoint Studio/Shutterstock Images
Interior Photos: Diana Grytsku/Shutterstock Images, 8; iStockphoto, 11, 15, 24–25, 36–37, 40, 44, 50, 54, 75, 85, 94; Wavebreak Media/Shutterstock Images, 12–13, 98; Dean Drobot/Shutterstock Images, 18; Luza Studios/iStockphoto, 20; Wunder Visuals/iStockphoto, 22–23; Antonio Guillem/iStockphoto, 26, 46; Prostock-Studio/Shutterstock Images, 30; Shutterstock Images, 33, 60, 62, 65, 90; Jacob Wackerhausen/iStockphoto, 34; Zinkevych/iStockphoto, 43; Franck Boston/Shutterstock Images, 53; Star Stock/Shutterstock Images, 57; Antonio Diaz/iStockphoto, 66; Odua Images/Shutterstock Images, 70; Rob Marmion/Shutterstock Images, 72; Image Source/iStockphoto, 76; Monkey Business Images/iStockphoto, 80; FatCamera/iStockphoto, 83, 93; South Agency/iStockphoto, 86; Pamela Joe McFarlane/iStockphoto, 96–97

Editor: Aubrey Zalewski
Series Designer: Nikki Nordby

Library of Congress Control Number: 2019954377
Publisher's Cataloging-in-Publication Data

Names: Huddleston, Emma, author.
Title: Healthy friendships / by Emma Huddleston
Description: Minneapolis, Minnesota : Abdo Publishing, 2021 | Series: Strong, healthy girls | Includes online resources and index.
Identifiers: ISBN 9781532192197 (lib. bdg.) | ISBN 9781098210090 (ebook)
Subjects: LCSH: Friendship in children--Juvenile literature. | Interpersonal conflict in adolescence--Juvenile literature. | Friendship--Sociological aspects--Juvenile literature. | Attitude (Psychology)--Juvenile literature.
Classification: DDC 155.533--dc23

CONTENTS

DR. AMANDA

Dr. Amanda J. Rose has always been interested in relationships. Our closest relationships can bring us incredible happiness, but when our relationships don't go well, life can be very hard. Different relationships are important at different stages of life, with friendships being especially important for adolescents. Dr. Amanda has been studying girls' friendships for more than 20 years, with more than 5,000 youth participating in her research projects.

Dr. Amanda grew up in Ohio and went to college at the Ohio State University, where she majored in psychology and minored in English. Her senior thesis was her first research project on adolescence. After graduating summa cum laude, Dr. Amanda went on to study developmental psychology at the University of Illinois at Urbana-Champaign. There she earned her master's degree and her doctorate. For her master's thesis and doctoral dissertation, she studied how girls and boys handle conflict in their friendships and how they support each other in times of stress.

In 1999, Dr. Amanda joined the faculty at the University of Missouri as a founding member of the Developmental Psychology Training Program in the Department of Psychological Sciences. Together with her students, she has conducted many research studies, with a focus on the benefits and challenges of girls' friendships. This research has been funded by the National Institute of Mental Health. During her time at the University of Missouri, Dr. Amanda has received many honors and awards, including an Early Scientific Achievement Award from the Society for Research in Child Development and a Kemper Fellowship for Excellence in Teaching, one of the highest teaching honors awarded at the University of Missouri.

Dr. Amanda lives in Columbia, Missouri, with her husband, her teenage daughter and son, and her yellow Labrador retriever, Charlie.

TAKE IT

FROM ME

Thinking about friendship often brings a smile to my face and a pang to my heart. I smile thinking of funny memories with friends, such as the time one of my friends tried skiing for the first time. She only made it a few feet down the hill before sliding on her back the rest of the way and laughing the whole way down. At the same time, thinking of friendship makes my heart long to be with friends whom I haven't seen in a while.

Friendship comes with many emotions for teen girls. Some feel giddy remembering fun times or shared jokes. Some feel a sense of longing for childhood friends who moved away or drifted apart. Some feel embarrassed or angry about a fight. Most of all, many girls feel grateful for true friends and for the love and support of friendship.

Friendship can be challenging. You may be unsure of how to end a friendship. You may struggle to trust others or be tempted to spill a friend's secret. You may compete against a friend in sports or wonder how you can be friends with a sister who drives you crazy. Talking to others can help you make the right choices during these complicated times.

No matter who you are or what friendships you have, you'll probably feel both the joys and stresses of friendship. But you can make it easier for yourself by realizing that you aren't alone. No matter how uncertain you may feel about making new friends or getting over a fight, I guarantee that many other girls have been in the same position.

Part of what makes friendship so rewarding is that it's personal. Everyone's friendships are unique. It takes time and effort to get to know someone who may become a close friend, but it's usually worth it. Friends can support you as you begin to develop into an adult. Life events such as starting high school, dealing with a parent's divorce, or dating someone for the first time can be surprising and often challenging. In some situations, you'll have to make tough decisions and answer difficult questions. Being honest with yourself will help you deal with moments that can feel difficult or awkward. And finding people who support you can make life a whole lot easier.

XOXO,
EMMA

CHAPTER ONE

BEING THE NEW GIRL

Have you ever moved to a new city or town? Walking into a new class or new school can be intimidating. Leaving friends behind can be heartbreaking. Joining a new club or team can be nerve racking. All these emotions are normal when you're going through a time of social changes.

Many girls find themselves as "the new girl" at some point in life. You may join a club, go to a new school, or hang out with a different set of friends. No matter whether your personality is outgoing or shy, feeling set apart as the new girl isn't easy. You may not immediately click with the people you meet. You might have to figure out the culture of your new setting. And opening yourself up to new people and expressing who you are takes courage.

It can be tempting to focus on old friends, especially if you're having trouble fitting in with a new group. You may want to stay quiet or fade into the background because you know

9

you have other friends. But consider taking a chance to meet someone new.

Technology makes it easy to stay in touch when friends are in different places. But don't let time on the phone or computer take away opportunities to meet someone new. Making friends is worth the effort.

> Being the
> new girl is an
> opportunity for
> a fresh start.

Being the new girl is an opportunity for a fresh start. You can leave a reputation behind. Or you can continue the same habits with confidence. If you had a reputation of rubbing your good grades in others' faces, you could change that and use your skills to tutor instead. If you know you're good at singing, you can confidently join the school choir and make friends there.

You don't need to rush into a friendship or group. Take your time meeting people to find where you fit best in your new social situation.

ERIN'S STORY

Erin tied the laces of her new shoes and stood up. She was wearing her lucky jeans. They had colorful stitching and were quite different from trendy jeans. But she didn't care what other people thought. Today was her first day of rehearsal

for the school play. She was excited to begin. She was finally following her dream of becoming an actress. But she was also a bit nervous. If she messed up a line or acted awkwardly, her mistakes would be on display for people to see. Plus, she didn't know any of the drama club members well, and she didn't want to embarrass herself in front of people she didn't know.

While brushing her teeth, Erin thought about the cast members. One of the senior members of the group came to mind. He had gotten the lead role in the play three years in a row. He had a strong voice and confident attitude. During last year's play, his microphone went out while he was on stage, but he didn't miss a beat. He finished the play without a mic, projecting his voice throughout the auditorium. Even people in the back could hear loud and clear. His performance was impressive—

most people couldn't do that. Erin thought about other people in the group and realized they had done several plays before too.

They're amazing actors. They have more experience and practice than me, Erin thought. *There is so much I don't know about performing . . .* Then Erin shook her head and stopped focusing on what she was nervous about. She took a deep breath and pushed rehearsal to the back of her mind. After all, she had a full day of school to get through first.

***

When Erin walked into the auditorium after school, her excitement increased. She saw the wide stage and tall curtains. Her footsteps sounded crisp as she walked down the aisle. She smiled at some drama kids when she got to the front of the stage. Some smiled back. Others kept a straight face or looked away when she made eye contact with them. Erin felt a flicker of insecurity. Then she remembered other people were probably nervous too, so she didn't let their reactions get her down. She found somewhere to sit and took off her backpack.

TALK ABOUT IT

= **Have you ever felt like the new girl? What emotions did you experience?**

= **Imagine giving advice to a younger girl about what to do in a new situation. What might help someone who is nervous or scared?**

= **Why might girls want to fit in? Do you think fitting in is a healthy goal? Why or why not?**

= **How can you stay positive when you're nervous or stressed?**

- How would you react if you smiled at someone and they didn't smile back? Why?

- What do you do to prepare for big days or competitions? What tips would you give someone else for their first day of a new experience?

- What can you do to make yourself feel comfortable when you're in a new setting?

Erin was more comfortable sitting by herself than trying to decide whom to sit with before she knew people. She saw small groups of friends forming and thought about whom she might get along with in the future. She hoped to find friends who were serious about rehearsal but also liked to have fun outside of practice. She saw a group of three friends across the room. One was studying a textbook while the others chatted and laughed. She thought they could be a good group to meet. But today, she enjoyed having a little time to herself.

Erin thought about how to start a conversation with someone. She saw a girl who was also sitting alone a few seats away and decided to talk to her.

"Hi, I'm Erin," she said, with a smile.

"Hi! I'm Beth. Are you new this year?"

"Yeah, this is my first play. Have you been in the school play before?"

"Oh yeah, I've done it every year," Beth replied.

"Cool! Which play was your favorite?" Erin asked. She and Beth talked for a few minutes, and then practice started. When the director asked whether anyone had memorized any lines yet,

Erin's hand was one of the few that went up. The question reminded her of one of her strengths: memorizing lines. Erin smiled. She belonged among the other talented cast members.

During breaks, Erin looked for Beth, who introduced her to more people. Not everyone was as friendly as Beth, but most offered a handshake or grin. At the end of the day, Erin waved goodbye to Beth. She left the auditorium feeling more comfortable and looking forward to making other friends as they got to know each other better.

TALK ABOUT IT

= **What are some ways to introduce yourself or start a conversation with someone you don't know?**

= **Besides joining a club, how else can you meet new people or make friends?**

= **If you notice a new kid, what can you do to make him or her feel welcome?**

EXPERT

Erin didn't worry about which clothes she wore or how other people reacted to her. She stayed true to herself on the first day of theater practice. She used positive self-talk to boost her confidence and remember her strengths.

Introducing yourself to someone you don't know can feel intimidating. But many girls underestimate how kind most people will be. And, who knows, maybe the person you talk to is feeling the exact same way you are. If you have a hard time starting a conversation, think of what to say in advance and practice. Often, people begin by stating their name. Then they break the ice. An icebreaker helps get the conversation going. Questions and compliments are commonly used to start conversations. Knowing what to say when meeting someone new can take some stress off your shoulders.

If you're ever a new girl, remember that it can take time to develop a close friendship. Often, the first step to friendship is spending time together. You'll get to know each other. Over time, you'll build trust and make memories. Whether you're new in town or live in the same place you always have, getting involved in clubs or neighborhood events is a great way to meet people who share your interests. And you'll have a natural way to spend time together too.

GET HEALTHY

- Keep a positive mindset. Focus on yourself and your strengths.

- Limit stress by separating what's in your control from what's not. You only can change what you can control.

- Try something new and introduce yourself to someone there. You can meet new people and make friends if you're willing to try.

- Resist the urge to act differently in order to fit in. Be yourself and you'll find friends who share your interests.

THE LAST WORD FROM EMMA

When I was the new girl in high school, I was nervous about finding friends. After telling my mom about my worries, she gave me an example of how I could start a conversation with someone. She suggested asking someone at lunch about upcoming events or the best classes. A question would give me a reason to meet someone new, and I could get the scoop about my new school too.

Being the new girl isn't easy, but you can make the best of it. I met my best friend when I asked her where to find the bathroom! The first conversation was slightly awkward. But we sat next to each other in a class and studied together. Eventually, we found topics besides school to talk about, and then we talked about everything. I was glad I changed schools because otherwise I never would have met her!

CHAPTER TWO

GETTING OVER A FIGHT

Fights break out between friends every day. Girls argue over who can wear a certain outfit to a school dance. Some compete in sports or for the attention of a crush. Friends disagree about what to do while they hang out. Sometimes friendships fall apart because of misunderstandings or false rumors.

Whether mundane or shocking, fights between friends are normal because every girl has her own opinions, personality, and point of view. Even though friends may get along most of the time, they are still different people and are bound to clash sometimes. They will never see things exactly the same way. Plus, no one acts her best or says the right things all the time.

Girls make mistakes as they grow up. For these reasons and more, learning to apologize and forgive your friends is an important part of teen friendship.

However, apologizing isn't always easy. It requires taking responsibility for what went wrong, and many people don't want to admit their faults. On the other hand, forgiveness can be difficult too. Close friends who abandon plans, insult you, or gossip behind your back can cause deep hurt. Choosing to give a friend another chance takes courage. As you navigate the bumpy road of friendship, learn to think and act carefully.

DIANA'S STORY

"Let's go to the new museum exhibit this Saturday!" Diana suggested to her friend Harper.

"You don't mean the space one, do you?" Harper asked, cringing.

"Well . . ." Diana blushed.

"Didn't you see the picture of it in the news? Planets hanging from the ceiling." Harper waved her arms as she spoke. "It looked like a school science fair. I don't want to feel like I'm at school on the weekend!" she said. "Any chance you would rather have a movie day?" Harper gave Diana a hopeful smile.

"I guess we could do that," Diana said. But Harper saw Diana's face fall.

"Forget it," Harper said. "Museum on Saturday, it is!"

"Yes!" Diana exclaimed.

***

Saturday started out great. Diana felt like she couldn't stop smiling all morning at the exhibit. Even though the line at the museum was long, Harper admitted that being part of the opening day crowd was a

TALK ABOUT IT

= **How can friends choose what to do in a fair way? How do you and your friends make plans?**

= **How can girls make sure friendly teasing doesn't go too far or hurt the other person's feelings? What should someone do if teasing does go too far?**

= **What are healthy ways for friends to get over small arguments or disagreements?**

neat experience. That afternoon, the girls decided to eat dinner at home and meet up again to watch some of Harper's movies.

Diana lounged on the couch with Harper, and they shared a warm blanket and popcorn. Suddenly, Diana's phone buzzed in her pocket. A notification with the words "Kristie's Bonfire" flashed on the screen. *Oh no!* Diana thought, holding the phone to her chest so Harper wouldn't see. Harper glanced at Diana but turned back to the screen when she saw Diana was just checking her phone. *I forgot that the bonfire was tonight!* Diana thought. *I can't miss it; Kristie is counting on me to come. But Harper will be upset if I bail on movie night.* Diana pretended to pay attention to the movie, but her mind raced as she tried to decide what to do.

After watching one movie, Diana faked feeling sick. She waved goodbye to Harper and went straight to the bonfire. *She can still watch another movie without me,* Diana thought, *and I won't have to miss the bonfire*

Oh no! Diana thought, holding the phone to her chest so Harper wouldn't see.

TALK ABOUT IT

- **How can friends balance doing activities that each person wants to do?**
- **Would you have made the same decision as Diana? What would you have done?**

23

or hurt Harper's feelings by telling her I have other plans. As she roasted a marshmallow and talked with Kristie, Diana was glad she didn't let her friends down.

***

"Glad you're feeling better," Harper said curtly when she saw Diana at school on Monday. "How was the bonfire? Kristie's post made it look great. I bet it was a blast," Harper added. She wasn't smiling.

"Harper, I didn't . . . I'm sorry!" Diana said. Harper walked ahead of her down the hallway. Diana followed. She wanted to apologize right away.

"I didn't tell you because I didn't want to hurt your feelings," Diana explained when she caught up to Harper at her locker. "I knew Kristie was counting on me to be at her party. I figured I'd watch a movie with you and then go to the bonfire. I could make it through Saturday without letting either of you down!" Harper didn't look convinced. "But I guess I was wrong."

Harper slammed her locker and looked at Diana. "If you don't want to hang out with me, just tell me."

> "I didn't tell you because I didn't want to hurt your feelings."

25

"I'm sorry," Diana said again. "You know I love hanging out with you, and I wish I could redo Saturday night."

"You didn't have to lie to me. I would have understood that you'd forgotten you had made other plans," Harper said. She still looked upset, but she didn't seem to be as mad.

"I know. I promise I won't do it again." Diana worried her apology wasn't enough.

Harper was silent for several seconds.

"OK, thanks. I have to get to class, but I'll see you later," Harper said.

***

Later that week, Diana was sitting at home on her couch when her phone buzzed. She looked and saw she had a text from Harper. They hadn't spoken much that week, so Diana quickly texted a reply. They texted back and forth for a few hours, and soon it felt like everything was back to normal. Then Diana texted, "Do you have plans this weekend? Maybe we could have another movie night."

Harper's reply seemed to take forever. Diana kept checking her phone. *Maybe she's still mad*, she thought. Her phone finally buzzed. It was from Harper.

"Sure. What should we watch?"

TALK ABOUT IT

- **What makes a good apology?**
- **How can someone decide whether to accept an apology?**
- **What should you do if a friend doesn't accept your apology or forgive you?**
- **Do you have any advice for people who often fight with a friend?**

EXPERT

Diana tried to make a decision that would please everyone, but Harper's feelings got hurt, and Diana couldn't take back what she did. After hearing Diana's apology, Harper decided to give her another chance. She didn't excuse what Diana did, but she trusted her friend wouldn't make the same mistake again.

Resolving a fight is about getting over a disagreement and finding a way to stay friends. It's also about learning to be respectful when your feelings may be hurt or when you're tempted to lash out. One important part of getting over a fight is listening to the other person's side of the story. Hearing someone's point of view often shows where things went wrong.

Getting defensive when a friend brings up a tough topic can easily cause a fight. Diana could have become defensive. She thought what she had done was the best for both of her friends. But instead, she recognized how her actions affected Harper. People who are defensive put their own thoughts and feelings above those of others. In order to grow as a person and overcome conflict, girls must be open to talking, apologizing, and forgiving. They must be willing to take responsibility for their actions instead of putting blame on others.

In the end, friends who get over a fight often have a stronger relationship than before. They know their friendship can handle ups and downs. They know that they want to forgive each other.

GET **HEALTHY**

- Don't let frustration build up. Talk with your friend about issues as they come up.
- Learn to listen. Many fights happen because of misunderstandings. Take time to listen to both sides of the story.
- Always be respectful. Disagreeing doesn't make it OK to say rude or hurtful things.
- Agree to disagree. Sometimes friends have different opinions, and they can still be friends.

THE LAST WORD FROM **EMMA**

When I was in high school, one of my friends threw a huge party for her sixteenth birthday. But I didn't get invited. I worried she left me out on purpose. I thought the lack of an invitation meant she didn't want to hang out with me. But a few days before the party, I learned that I was accidentally left out. She thought she had sent me a text message, but she typed in the wrong number!

Overthinking a situation can negatively affect a friendship. It can cause girls to not trust each other or to imagine additional problems. You can keep friendships strong by focusing on honesty and trust. Telling friends the truth and believing what others have to say can help you avoid misunderstandings. And when disagreements happen, you can apologize and look for a solution instead of dwelling on the issue.

CHAPTER THREE

TOUGH TIMES

You'll likely experience physical, mental, and emotional changes during your teen years. You may get sick or injured during the middle of a sports season. Or you might struggle in school and have to retake classes to catch up. You may experience heartbreak for the first time. On top of dealing with your own problems, changes in the lives of your loved ones and the world around you can affect your life as well. Unfortunately, we don't always have control over what happens. All of us need support in tough times.

Research shows that true friends are good for your health. They help your body by lowering stress levels and encouraging healthy lifestyle habits, such as exercising. They benefit your mind by increasing your happiness, positivity, confidence, and ability to cope. Making friendships last takes effort. True friends listen to each other, go out of their way to help, and push each other to be the best they can be. Being a friend to someone who is struggling takes extra care and attention. But supporting someone you love is important because it makes them feel valued.

Adolescence can be a difficult time in a girl's life. Jade learned that Allie needed a friend she could count on as she dealt with stress in other areas of her life.

JADE'S STORY

Jade waved wildly out her car window at her best friend, Allie, in the parking lot at school. Allie seemed to notice her but quickly looked away. Jade immediately stopped waving and dropped her arms. In the hallway, she decided to ask Allie what was going on.

"Why didn't you wave back at me outside?"

"I didn't see you," Allie said, shrugging. Her face looked blank.

"Oh, it seemed like you did, but OK. How's it going today?" Jade wanted to brighten Allie's mood. She seemed down about something.

"Um, fine. I didn't sleep well, and I'm worried about that bio test."

"Yeah, me too. Maybe we can study together tonight," Jade suggested.

"Let's go to your house," Allie said. Jade was surprised. They usually went to Allie's house.

"Sure, I'll text my parents." Jade smiled, and Allie gave her a quick half smile before they went their separate ways to class.

Jade noticed Allie wasn't acting like herself. *Did I say something to hurt her feelings?* Jade thought as she walked. She hoped Allie would feel

TALK ABOUT IT

▪ **When a friend doesn't answer you, how do you respond and why?**

▪ **How can you show you care and try to understand why a friend is hurting without being annoying or prying?**

▪ **How can you help a friend when she is feeling stressed?**

better after studying tonight. Maybe she really was just stressed about the test.

***

That night at Jade's house, Jade and Allie sat next to each other at the kitchen table. They had textbooks open, pencils in hand, and lots of notes in front of them. They took turns quizzing each other. Suddenly, Allie's phone rang. She got up quickly and went to another room to answer it.

That's odd, Jade thought. Usually the girls just spoke on the phone in front of each other. When Allie came back in the room a few minutes later, Jade saw tears in her eyes.

"Allie? Is everything OK? Who was that?"

"It was just my dad. He's fine, but I . . ." Allie began to cry. "My parents are splitting up. They're getting a divorce." She wiped her eyes on her sleeve. Jade put her arm around her friend, and Allie's head fell onto her shoulder. "I just found out last night. I couldn't sleep, and today, I couldn't stop thinking about how much is going to change."

"Allie, I'm so sorry," Jade said. She and Allie sat for a few minutes without talking. Jade thought about the time she broke her arm and Allie sat with her in the hospital waiting room. Allie told her stories and jokes to keep her mind off of the pain in her arm. Allie's distractions were just what she needed. Now, Jade wondered what she could do to help her friend through this tough time.

"I don't know what you're feeling, but let me know if there's any way I can help," Jade said.

"Thanks," Allie replied.

TALK ABOUT IT

= Look at Jade's response to Allie after Allie explained what was happening in her life. How might the conversation have been different if Jade said "I understand" instead of "I don't know what you're feeling"?

= Listening to a friend share her feelings or a difficult story makes her feel heard. What behavior makes someone a good listener?

= What could you say or do to support a friend who's upset?

35

Allie was quiet for a few minutes. She didn't seem to want to talk about her parents anymore. Jade decided to make plans for dinner because they hadn't eaten.

"Hey," Jade said, "what should we eat for dinner? Pizza?"

"Sure, sounds good to me," Allie agreed.

TALK ABOUT IT

= **How would you want your friends to treat you if you were going through a tough time?**

= **Do you think humor helps during difficult times? Why or why not?**

Jade was glad to see her true smile.

Jade looked up the pizza place's phone number and called. When she heard someone pick up the phone, she spoke right away.

"Hi, I would like to order a cheese pizza, please."

"I think you have the wrong number. This is a hair salon," a voice on the other end said.

"Oh, I'm sorry! Bye!" Jade hung up and burst out laughing. "I just tried to order a pizza from a hair salon!" she told Allie.

Allie laughed too, and the stress disappeared from her face. She looked relieved, and Jade was glad to see her true smile.

EXPERT

Instead of taking Allie's behavior personally, Jade realized Allie was hurting. Allie needed time to process the change taking place in her family. Jade wanted to be there for Allie because Allie had supported her in the past. That's what true friends do.

Approximately half of the kids in the United States see their parents break up. And divorce is just one example of how life can change. Other physical, mental, and emotional challenges also take a toll.

During any difficult time, you have to learn how to cope. The first step is naming what you're feeling and accepting it. Being sad, angry, disappointed, excited, or embarrassed is normal. You shouldn't avoid feeling different emotions. Instead, you can learn to express your feelings. Healthy ways to take care of yourself can include writing, exercising, or talking with a trusted friend.

There's no one way to help a friend through tough times. Sometimes your friend might welcome your advice. But other times, your friend might need space to be alone. She might even take out her negative feelings on you. She might act irritated, uninterested, or just not as nice as usual. If you think she's acting this way because she's going through a tough time, consider letting it slide. She may need you to be the bigger person.

Sometimes, a friend may need professional support. She may feel depressed, confused, or scared. She may feel that there is nothing she can do to make things better. Doctors, counselors, and therapists can give girls who are struggling with serious stress the help they need.

GET HEALTHY

- Remember that all people make mistakes. Sometimes friends say or do something hurtful because they are stressed, not because they are upset with you.
- Show you care. When a friend is struggling, your kind actions and words can make a big difference.
- Reach out for help or take friends seriously when they need help.
- Take time to think through what's going on in your life. You should be honest about how you feel and what you need.

THE LAST WORD FROM EMMA

I went through a hard time in high school when I injured my leg. I couldn't play on the soccer team and had to sit out of practice for weeks. My body was hurting. I was frustrated because I was weaker than usual. Plus, I was jealous of my teammates, who were able to continue playing.

Eventually I recovered and was able to play soccer again. The whole situation helped me develop empathy. So, when one of my friends was injured later that season, I had a greater understanding of what it was like to be in that position. I empathized with her experience and tried to support her until she healed.

CHAPTER FOUR

MANY FRIENDS

How many friends do you have? That question can be tough to answer because the word *friend* refers to a variety of relationships. Good friends are people who have shared life experiences together. Longtime friends can be separated or not talk for a while, but when they get back together, they feel like they never missed a beat. Family friends may include cousins you only see during holidays or reunions. Acquaintances are often people you know but aren't close with. You may see them by chance in your community. No matter the type of relationship, friends are a valuable part of life.

Besides making life fun, studies show that friends influence the type of person you become. Having close friends can help you live longer. For example, they can benefit your physical health by decreasing your chance of disease by lowering heart rate and blood pressure. Of course, friends also influence your choices. Sometimes friends give you support when you're trying to reach a goal. A strong-willed friend can help you develop discipline and self-control. Other times, they're your partners in crime when you need a break. But friends can also influence you in negative ways. If a friend blows off homework or acts disrespectfully toward adults, you may find yourself acting that way too—even if you didn't do that before you met the friend. For these reasons, choose your friends carefully.

> Girls can choose anyone to be friends with, but they should remember that friendship takes time and effort.

Girls can choose anyone to be friends with, but they should remember that friendship takes time and effort. A girl can't be best friends with everyone, but she can benefit from being kind to all the people in her social world.

KEELY'S STORY

"Tomorrow we will start group projects, so don't forget to brainstorm your own idea for discussion," the history teacher, Mr. Adelman, said.

Keely packed her bag and left. She was assigned to the same group project as Lin. Lin had recently transferred to the school.

They had a couple of classes together, but Keely had never spoken to her. Keely knew Lin was shy and smart, but they hung out with different friend groups.

At lunch, Keely noticed that Lin's usual friends were gone and that she was sitting by herself. So, Keely decided to invite her to eat at her table.

"Hey, Lin. We have US history together. I don't think we've talked before, but, uh, would you like to eat lunch over there with me?" Keely asked.

"Um, OK, thanks," Lin responded. She grabbed her food and followed Keely. As they sat down, Keely realized she wasn't sure

- Do you have a certain group of friends that you always hang out with, or do you float between friend groups? What are benefits or challenges of both situations?

- Have you ever invited someone to join your friend group or sit with you at lunch? Why is including others meaningful?

- How can a girl start a conversation with someone she doesn't know yet? Do you have any specific examples or advice?

how to start a conversation with Lin.

Since she and Lin were in the same class, Keely thought that would be a good topic to start with.

"So, what do you think about Mr. Adelman?" Keely asked Lin.

"He seems pretty cool. Do you like him?"

"Yeah, I had him for World Civilizations last year. He's one

of my favorite teachers," Keely said. She took a bite of her salad and tried to think of a new topic they could talk about. She was about to compliment Lin's jean jacket, but Lin spoke first.

"I love your backpack; it's a really cute color. Where did you get it?" Lin asked.

"Oh, thanks! I've had it forever; I don't really remember where I got it. Probably online somewhere—like everything else I buy," Keely said, with a laugh. The girls smiled at each other. They talked about their favorite stores, classes, movies, and celebrities. Before they knew it, lunch period was over.

***

Over the next weeks and months, Keely and Lin talked often. At first it was just during class when they worked on their group project. Then they sat together at lunch most days. They never hung out outside of school, but they enjoyed chatting with each other. Lin was unlike most of Keely's other friends. For example, when Keely wore her favorite skirt, Lin half-jokingly commented, "I hope you have shorts on under that!" Keely had owned the skirt for years, and she hadn't realized how short it was getting. She was glad Lin was honest instead of just complimenting her clothes to be nice.

TALK ABOUT IT

- What do you talk about with your friends?

- How are your conversations different based on whom you're talking to?

***

"Aw," Keely said. "Now we can't eat lunch together. We'll have to find some other time to talk."

"So after we finished shopping, my friends and I randomly decided to get haircuts," Keely told Lin. They were talking about what they did over the weekend. "What do you think? Is it too short?" Keely flipped her hair from side to side.

"No! I think it looks great!" Lin said, with a laugh.

"I could never just cut my hair on a whim, but that's totally your personality." She took a sip of her water and smiled at Keely.

"Well, yeah, but I could never just join the school band. How's that going, by the way?"

"It's lots of work," Lin said. She blushed and shrugged. "Actually, we have a concert coming up. Starting next week, I won't be eating at this time anymore because of extra band practice."

"Aw," Keely said. "Now we can't eat lunch together. We'll have to find some other time to talk."

"Yeah, definitely!" Lin said.

"If I'm free the day of your concert, I'll come see how good you are!" Keely smiled.

The lunch bell rang, and the girls walked to the cafeteria door together. Then they parted ways.

"See you around!" Lin said.

"See ya!" Keely waved.

TALK ABOUT IT

■ Is there someone in your life whom you see regularly but don't often speak with? Why do you think you don't speak? Do you wish you spoke more?

■ Why do you think Keely and Lin can comfortably talk about other friends in front of each other?

■ Do you think acquaintance friendships are worthwhile? Why or why not?

ASK THE

EXPERT

Keely and Lin were acquaintances who became friends. They enjoyed sitting together at lunch and getting one another's opinion about hairstyles and clothes. However, both girls had separate friend groups and best friends they saw outside of school. Keely and Lin's lunchtime conversations were ending, but now that they were more comfortable together, it didn't mean their friendship had to end.

Anthropologist Robin Dunbar is known for doing social studies. In one study, he found that most people have a connection to about 150 people. That number includes a range of connections, including a person's best friend as well as more distant acquaintances. Dunbar's theory categorizes friendship into four levels. On average, people have three to five very personal relationships, or best friends. Then, they have approximately 15 close relationships with more family and friends. Next, they have up to 50 connections with other friends. Finally, the largest level includes acquaintances or familiar faces from your community.

Most of all, Dunbar's theory emphasizes that every level matters. Having close and more distant friends makes for a well-rounded social life. Sometimes people move from one level to another at certain points in life. That helps people learn to manage different friendships.

GET **HEALTHY**

- Fill your social circle with different kinds of friends. You can have lots of friends throughout your life, and you don't have to be best friends with everyone.

- Be kind to everyone. Consider asking someone new to join your friend group or be extra friendly to an acquaintance.

- Be ready for changing friendships. As you get older, it's natural for some friendships to get closer and others to become more distant.

- Don't be afraid to reach out to an old friend. Maybe you parted ways with a friend years ago, but that doesn't mean your friendship has to be over.

THE LAST WORD FROM **EMMA**

In middle school, I wondered if I was weird because I didn't have a best friend. Television shows I watched and books I read defined best friends as girls who hung out after school each day and sometimes wore the same clothes. Instead of that type of friendship, I was connected to different groups of friends through school, sports, and my church. I saw some friends more than others, but I still felt like each friendship was special in its own way.

One day I told my mom that I was worried about finding a "best friend." She reminded me that having different kinds of friends is healthy, and every girl's circle of friends is unique. Her advice was just what I needed to hear. I didn't need to worry. I learned that having multiple friends was normal, especially when I had lots of fun with each friend group.

CHAPTER FIVE

BEING A FRIEND AND A SISTER

Many girls have sisters. They may share a room or live in different homes. Some are stepsisters or half sisters. Some sisters are twins or triplets. Others are much older or younger than their sisters. Friendship comes easy to some sisters, and it's a challenge for others. No matter how close sisters are, getting along is helpful because they will always be family.

Learning to balance a friendship between sisters isn't easy. Spending too much time together can cause fights or competitions. Being compared with a sister can lead to jealousy or low self-esteem. Arguing with each other or with parents about what's fair can create distance between sisters. But sisters

> They find ways to compromise and respect each other when they disagree.

can help each other become better people. They can set rules for sharing. They find ways to compromise and respect each other when they disagree. By listening to each other, they help each other understand the other person's perspective.

Sisters are true friends when they support each other, help each other reach goals, and make time for fun during stressful times. Sisterhood can be a bumpy road, but sisters who love each other can eventually learn how to be friends too.

ROSE'S STORY

"Maddie! I've got to brush my teeth *now*! I can't be late! I have a test in my first class!" Rose yelled through the bathroom door.

"One *second*!" her younger sister, Maddie, answered. Then Maddie opened the door. "Hey, is that my jacket?" She crossed her arms over her chest. "You never asked to borrow it."

"Sorry, I was busy studying, and I forgot. Can I borrow it? Please, please, please?" Rose begged. Maddie was just a year and a half younger than Rose and was basically the same size. On any other day, Rose would shrug off the jacket, but not today.

She was already stressed about being late for her test, and she really hoped Maddie would show her mercy.

"Fine," Maddie said, and stomped back to her room.

"Thanks!" Rose answered sweetly. Then she used her serious voice again: "We still need to leave in five minutes!"

***

When the school bell rang at the end of the day, Rose walked to the car with a grin on her face. Maddie came walking out of school with a big smile too.

TALK ABOUT IT

■ How can relationships with family members be more complicated than other friendships?

■ Can you think of any rules or systems that would help girls who live together avoid fights?

■ Should sisters use manners around each other? Why or why not?

53

"Woo! Done with my last test of the year!" Rose said. She threw her bag in the trunk and closed the lid with a *thud*. "Only one day before summer vacation. I'm not going to look at a single textbook for the whole summer." Maddie laughed. She plopped into the passenger seat. She had taken her last test of the year the day before.

"Let's get ice cream to celebrate," Maddie said. Rose got in the car and turned the key. She nodded.

"Great idea."

The girls drove down the street and talked about plans for the summer.

"I want to go hiking. I think you would love this place I drove past last week," Rose said.

"Oh great! I'd love to practice photography in the woods with all the trees and flowers. But the camera I want is expensive. I need to make some money. Do you have any ideas?"

"You could always babysit; you're great with kids. Or we could make jewelry and sell it online!" Rose suggested.

"Good idea! We can split the money if you want to help," Maddie said.

"No, you don't have to pay me. It'll be fun!" Rose responded. She parked the car, and the girls got out. "But you still have to buy your own ice cream today." She smiled, and the girls laughed as they walked into the shop.

***

After ice cream, the girls decided to stop by the hiking spot Rose mentioned. Maddie immediately began talking about how the bluff in the distance would make a beautiful backdrop for some wide shots of the whole area. She had an eye for picturesque scenes.

TALK ABOUT IT

- **Why do you think sisters sometimes get along but other times don't?**

- **How can sisters support each other's interests?**

- **How can spending time together affect sisters' relationships?**

Rose had an eye for detail.

On the other hand, Rose had an eye for detail. She walked down the beginning of the trail and pointed out neat close-up shots Maddie could take with her new camera.

"You know, if you help me make money to buy a camera, I suppose you could use it a few times too," Maddie said hesitantly.

"Really?" Rose raised her eyebrows. Maddie was really protective of the camera she currently had.

"Yeah. It seems like you could be good at it."

"Well, thanks! That'd be sweet!" Rose was excited. "Let's get home and think up jewelry designs!" she said, only half joking.

"You know we'll have to do chores first," Maddie said.

"Yeah, yeah, don't remind me."

***

After dinner, Rose was feeling a bit tired and didn't feel like doing chores. Maddie wasn't in the mood either.

"No, you do it. I swept the floor last week," Rose said and pushed the broom toward her sister.

"Mom said I get first pick on chores this week, and I picked taking out the garbage," Maddie responded.

"That's not fair!" Rose shouted. "I offered to help you make money this summer, and you repay me by picking the chore that only takes a minute."

"Oh, c'mon, you would do the same thing."

"Whatever you say . . ." Rose shrugged and raised her eyebrows. Her look made Maddie's cheeks turn red. Maddie walked out of the room, and Rose heard a bedroom door slam.

TALK ABOUT IT

= Is it possible to make every situation completely fair? If yes, how? If not, what should a girl do when she feels she is being treated unfairly?

= How can sisters respect each other even when they are upset?

ASK THE

EXPERT

Rose helped Maddie when she came up with ideas for making money to buy a camera. And Maddie showed Rose she cared when she offered to let Rose use her new camera. The sisters loved each other, and they often enjoyed spending time together. But that didn't stop them from getting frustrated or upset.

Sister relationships often face challenges. They may have to deal with family issues. The girls' individual personalities may be different and clash. Sisters often rival each other for space, attention, or items at home. One sister may feel left out or treated unfairly compared to the other. Learning to balance *me time* with *we time* can be hard for sisters to figure out.

However, careful attention and effort can go a long way. Sisters often know each other well because they live together. They can choose to use their knowledge to help or hurt their relationship. For example, if you know your sister is nervous about a test, helping her study shows you want her to succeed and feel prepared.

Many sisters share special moments such as late-night talks and family vacations. They can enjoy weekend activities and life events together. These experiences can create a deep bond between sisters. They see each other in good times and bad as they grow from children to adults. Having a sister to support you through life can be one of the best relationships you have.

GET **HEALTHY**

- Sisters need to spend time alone and together. Alone time lets you focus on yourself and your needs. Spending time together shows you care and helps your relationship grow.
- Don't compare yourself to a sister or a friend. You are an individual with your own personality and skills.
- Life is not perfectly fair. Compromising or creating a system to solve a problem is better than complaining or arguing.
- Apologize and forgive each other. Everyone makes mistakes, and sisters often see each other make mistakes while growing up.

THE LAST WORD FROM **EMMA**

I grew up with two sisters, and our relationships were very different. One sister is much younger than I am, and when she was a baby, I sometimes felt like her mom. But I always enjoyed playing with her and supporting her whenever she needed help.

My other sister was so close in age and appearance to me that many of our relatives confused us even when we were in high school. She and I had a sibling rivalry growing up. We shared a room and fought over who had to clean it. We got jealous of toys or clothes that the other had, and we often competed for our parents' attention. But when we were teens, we realized we wanted to focus on friendship. We've shared countless special memories together, and that makes it easier to be patient with each other.

CHAPTER SIX

KEEPING SECRETS

Friends keep many kinds of secrets for each other. They throw surprise parties. They know about each other's crushes. They know whether someone fears heights or snakes more. You can strengthen a friendship by sharing secrets with someone. On the other hand, you can cause problems or ruin a friendship if you spill a friend's secrets. Learning to trust others and be trustworthy in return makes you a true friend.

During adolescence, girls get closer with friends who share their interests, and they figure out which friends they can trust. Little by little, girls learn what it is like to be intimate with another person as they share secrets and take the risk of counting on someone else.

Overall, your friends should be people you can talk to when you're struggling or dealing with challenges. Having someone to confide in gives you mental and emotional support. Laura and

Ash both trusted each other with secrets and realized the value of trusted friends.

LAURA'S STORY

The school was throwing a Valentine's Day dance in two weeks. Some teachers had red streamers hanging from their doorways. Others drew hearts on the classroom whiteboards. Laura and Ash were both excited about the dance.

"What are you going to wear?" Laura asked. "I can't tell if the dance is meant to be casual or formal."

"Whatever I wear, I know it will be red," Ash said. "But the bigger question is who we're going with."

"Yeah . . . " Laura paused, thinking. "Well, we're obviously not going with dates. Our crushes don't even know we like them!" Ash agreed, and the girls laughed.

Ash was gay, but she hadn't come out publicly yet. Only her parents and Laura knew. If they had chosen to go with dates, Ash would've been faced with some big—and possibly awkward—decisions.

> Ash was gay, but she hadn't come out publicly yet.

"Let's just go with a group," Laura said. "I'll message the group chat now and see if any of the girls have plans yet." Soon, they heard multiple *pings* as girls responded.

"Oh, it looks like everyone else has a date," Ash said. "Maybe we should too?"

"But who would you go with?"

TALK ABOUT IT

- When you have a secret, whom do you tell? Why?

- How do you know whether you can trust a friend with a big secret?

- How might not telling something to a trusted friend change your relationship?

"I don't know . . . " Ash said as she looked down.

"We can still go with each other," Laura said. "We had so much fun at the last dance, and people just go with dates to take pictures. They don't usually stay with their date the whole night."

"Yeah, you're right," Ash said. "We better make sure our outfits don't clash in our pictures," she joked.

"Do you want to go with a date? I could help you find one!"

***

The next day, Laura and Ash sat with their friends at lunch. The conversation was centered on plans for the school dance. Some girls talked about what to wear. Others were figuring out the time and location for pictures. When the girls started talking about dates, Laura and Ash were asked lots of questions.

TALK ABOUT IT

- **What can you do when friends bombard you with personal or uncomfortable questions?**
- **How can you politely respond to people when you don't want to answer their questions?**

"Do you want to go with a date? I could help you find one!"

"Who do you have a crush on? We could get him to go with you!"

"C'mon, you've got to like somebody! Tell us!"

64

Laura and Ash shrugged off each question.

"We don't really want to go with dates," Laura said.

"But thanks for offering," Ash added.

***

Later, Laura was at her locker alone. She traded out some textbooks and notebooks. Then, one of the girls from lunch came up to her.

"Hey, Laura," Crystal said. "So, I know that you and Ash said you were OK going alone, but don't you think it would be nice to

surprise Ash with a date? I mean, you know who she likes, so what if you just tell me? Then we can secretly work together. I think it would be a sweet thing to do for Ash, don't you think?"

Laura knew Crystal meant well, and telling Ash's secret might boost her friendship with Crystal. But Laura also knew Ash's secret wasn't hers to tell, and she didn't want to have a reputation for spilling secrets. She decided to change the subject.

"That's sweet of you, but if Ash wanted a date, she would tell us. Hey, do you know what you're going to wear? I haven't decided yet."

"Oh, you're probably right. And yeah, I already bought my dress. It's this shimmery emerald color that I'm completely in love with. You know, I have a dress that I wore at Christmas that would be really cute on you, if you want to borrow it."

"That would be great! Thanks!" Laura said. "Maybe we can get ready for the dance together too. Do you have plans yet?"

"Yes, let's do that! I was just going to ask you and Ash if you wanted to come over to my house to get ready. Come over around three o'clock?" Crystal offered.

"Fun, I'll be there," Laura said and waved as she walked to class.

TALK ABOUT IT

= How do you decide when to share or keep a secret?

= Are there any times when it is necessary to tell a friend's secret? Why or why not?

= Sometimes it can be difficult not to spill a friend's secrets. Do you have advice for other girls in similar situations?

ASK THE

EXPERT

Laura and Ash weren't worried about fitting in when they went to the dance. They were comfortable going together. Laura showed she had Ash's best interests in mind when she encouraged her not to rush making decisions about finding a date. In the end, Laura could have spilled Ash's secret, but keeping it showed she was a true friend.

Additionally, Ash's secret was about more than just a crush. Ash hadn't come out about her sexual orientation yet, and she deserved to control the timing of when she told others. If Laura had spread the news that Ash was gay without Ash's permission, it would have been incredibly hurtful to Ash.

Sharing a friend's secret with someone else breaks trust. Trust is one of the keys to a strong, healthy friendship. When girls know they can trust each other with secrets big and small, they can find comfort in friends. They can talk to each other about personal questions or dilemmas, and they have someone to confide in.

GET HEALTHY

- Keep secrets a secret, with one exception. If you learn someone is in danger of harm, you should talk to an adult. Getting help and keeping others safe is crucial.

- Be honest and respectful. Trust and support at all times are keys to a strong friendship.

- Open up to others once you get to know them. Girls who have someone to confide in benefit mentally and emotionally.

- Remember your reputation. Based on your actions, you can be known for spilling secrets or for being a trustworthy friend.

THE LAST WORD FROM EMMA

Not only can spilling secrets hurt your relationship with a friend but it can also lead to problems with future friends. Drama may spread. Telling a secret that's not yours can cause other issues in your friend group. Girls may be reluctant to get close to you if you're known for gossiping or telling other people's secrets.

On the other hand, some girls are known for being completely trustworthy. I was lucky to have a close friend who would never tell a secret. She kindly shook her head or even walked away when people pressed her to tell information. When I asked her if she was ever tempted to spill a secret, she told me, "No, it's easy to keep secrets for friends because they're worth more to me than any gossip."

CHAPTER SEVEN

DIFFERENT BACKGROUNDS

A Muslim girl wears a head scarf that covers her hair, ears, and neck. The head scarf is a sign of modesty. An African American girl lights a black candle to celebrate the beginning of Kwanzaa. She gathers with her family around the candle to talk. A girl of Chinese heritage attends Chinese New Year celebrations. She smiles as many paper lanterns light up the night.

Each girl has her own personality, family, and culture. Her culture is made of traditions and beliefs. It affects her way of life. The places she's lived, the people she grew up with, and her own likes and dislikes have shaped her into the person she is. For this reason, some girls dress, act, and speak differently from you. But that doesn't mean you can't become great friends.

Friends can positively influence you. The positive influence from a multicultural friendship can affect other relationships. You may be less likely to judge someone at first glance. And you may be more likely to give others a second chance. Being open to diverse ideas can help you become a better person and friend.

CHRISTINE'S STORY

"It's beautiful!" Marta's mom exclaimed.

Christine was at her friend Marta's house while Marta tried on her quinceañera dress for her fifteenth birthday celebration. Marta looked like royalty.

"I can't wait!" Marta agreed. "I think the doughnut wall is going to be my favorite part."

"Oh yeah, I love doughnuts," Christine agreed. Marta and Christine had been friends for a few years. They met at a summer tennis camp, and now they played together on the high school team. The girls first bonded over their love of professional tennis star Serena Williams. Christine was black and especially looked up to Williams, who had made history as a black woman in a white-dominated sport.

"I'm looking forward to the Mass and seeing all our relatives," Marta's mother said. "OK, let's get you out of the dress, and I'll hang it back in the bag until the big day." She smiled and helped Marta change. Marta looked at Christine with pure excitement.

"You're going to look so gorgeous," Christine gushed. "I noticed you have two pairs of shoes. Have you decided which ones you're going to wear?"

Marta laughed. "No, I'm not trying to choose between them. I'm going to wear both! It's part of the tradition."

"Oh, oops," Christine said, and she blushed. "So, uh, what's the tradition exactly?"

"Changing from flat shoes to high heels is a symbol of my becoming a woman," Marta

"I noticed you have two pairs of shoes."

TALK ABOUT IT

- Have you ever misunderstood a cultural tradition? If so, how did you feel, and what did you do in the situation? If not, how might you have felt?

- Christine learned the meaning behind a tradition by asking a friend from that culture. Where else can you learn about other traditions and cultures?

- Do you think friends should be expected to know about each other's cultures? Why or why not?

explained. "That idea is pretty much the theme of the day."

"Got it," Christine said quickly. She was still a little embarrassed that she didn't know about the tradition. Christine's phone rang. "Oh, my stepdad's calling me. I've gotta go. I'll see you at school!" Christine said and made her way to the door.

"Bye!" Marta said.

***

Christine folded laundry and put it away. Marta was coming over soon to watch a movie. While she worked, Christine thought about Marta's upcoming party. She was nervous to go. She had never been to a quinceañera before. Not only was she unfamiliar with some of the traditions but she might not get to spend much time with Marta. *Maybe I won't go*, Christine thought. *I could just see her pictures and listen to her talk about it afterward.*

Then the doorbell rang. Marta had arrived.

"Only a few more days until the party!" Marta said. "Are you excited? Have you picked out what you're going to wear?"

"Uh, actually, I was just thinking about it," Christine confessed. "And I'm really excited for you! But I don't know if I should go after all. I mean, I'm not one of your family members . . ." Christine fidgeted with her hands. She crossed and uncrossed her arms.

"Oh," Marta said. She looked hurt. "I don't want to force you to come, I guess."

"No! That's not it!" Christine didn't want Marta thinking the wrong thing. "Never mind, I'm going to come. I just got nervous because I've never been to one before," Christine said.

= **Have you ever been invited to or gone to an event that made you nervous? What did you do?**

= **How can you support your friends when they have traditions that are different from yours?**

She realized she was being ridiculous. She liked Marta and wanted to support her, so she was definitely going to her party—even at the risk of a little discomfort.

76

"Really?" Marta's eyes lit up. "I'm so glad! It just wouldn't be the same without you," she said.

***

At Marta's quinceañera, Christine was nervous, but she got more comfortable as the party went on. She didn't know most of the people there, but she cheered with the other guests as Marta and her Court of Honor performed an impressively choreographed dance together. When Christine chatted with some of Marta's cousins, she learned that Marta would be receiving a last doll. Like the heels, this would symbolize her becoming an adult. Christine looked around the buzzing reception hall. She could tell from the smiles on people's faces that everyone was enjoying this celebration of Marta.

Christine grabbed a couple doughnuts and handed one to Marta. "Cheers!" Christine said, raising a doughnut in the air.

"Cheers!" Marta replied, tapping her doughnut on Christine's. The girls laughed and took a bite at the same time.

TALK ABOUT IT

- Do you think everyone should experience events and traditions from other cultures? Why or why not?
- How can friends respect each other's traditions?
- How can going out of your comfort zone benefit you?

ASK THE

EXPERT

Marta's cultural traditions were unfamiliar to Christine. Christine felt embarrassed when she misunderstood the shoe tradition, and she was tempted to avoid the quinceañera altogether. But she didn't want to hurt her friend. She realized supporting Marta mattered more than her fears or discomfort about experiencing something new.

Being open to others' cultures and backgrounds is important for all girls. For example, in the United States, there is no official language. Many people speak English, but as of 2017 about 20 percent of people speak a language besides English at home. Language is just one part of a person's culture, and it can create a barrier to communication. On the other hand, language differences can be a chance for friends to communicate in new ways and grow closer.

When learning about someone else's culture, it's normal to feel uncomfortable or unsure. In fact, feeling uncomfortable is a natural part of growing up. As girls experience new things and meet new people, they gain new understanding. Their knowledge of other practices and beliefs grows.

Having a wide range of friends helps you become more open and accepting of others. Instead of judging people from first glance, you may be more likely to get to know them. Friends of diverse backgrounds, beliefs, and lifestyles help you develop as an individual, and they show that kindness can connect all people.

GET **HEALTHY**

- Be respectful! Treat others with kindness and dignity no matter what.

- Reach out. Consider making a new friend with someone who has a different background from yours.

- Instead of making assumptions, just ask a friend to tell you about her culture. You can also do your own research.

- Have an open mind. Exploring other places or trying new foods are a couple of ways you can broaden your experiences with different cultures.

THE LAST WORD FROM **EMMA**

In high school, I wrote for the school newspaper. One year, I was assigned to write about the school talent show. The act that stood out to me was a few girls who did a traditional Indian dance. I had never seen a dance like it before and wanted to learn more. Later that week, I talked to the girls who performed the dance and learned a lot. I didn't realize the stereotypes I had in my head about their culture. For example, I thought there was one Indian dance style, called Bollywood dance. But Bollywood dance actually has elements of several Indian dance variations. We bonded over the topic of dance because I was a ballet dancer. Connecting and having a conversation with these girls who were from a different background than me opened my eyes to things I didn't know and how much more I had to learn.

CHAPTER EIGHT

TEAMMATES AND FRIENDS

Being part of a team has its ups and downs. Performing well or winning a competition is satisfying, and sometimes fun practices are full of laughter. Other times, having a bad competition or losing members of the group can really bring the mood down. Girls may blame each other for mistakes, start rumors, or fight.

Life on a team can be unpredictable. Referees call out foul plays or do-overs. Opponents bring different skills and tests to each game. Your health or the weather could affect the way you perform. However, the fast-paced social setting of a team sport offers many opportunities. You learn to work together and depend on the members of your team to do their individual parts. At the same time, you take responsibility for your role on the team. You can use your strengths to help the group in a competition, and everyone can be proud of what they accomplish.

Competition helps girls learn to deal with stress, and friends can help each other be their best. Teammates spend lots of time together. They may share physical challenges such as a difficult exercise or mental challenges such as an unfair loss. Hearing a friend cheer for you can give you a positive attitude or keep you focused on the game. Teammates often motivate one another to work hard. Seeing a friend spend extra time practicing can inspire another girl to do extra work herself.

It's normal for team dynamics to change from day to day. Staying positive and processing difficult moments is easier when you have a friend to share the ups and downs with. One of the most common reasons youth play sports is to be with friends or meet new ones. Teammates encourage each other during tough practices and unite against opponents. They make hard work worth it. And the friendships you make with your team can last longer than a game or season.

Hearing a friend cheer for you can give you a positive attitude or keep you focused on the game.

MALLORY'S STORY

Smack! Mallory hit the volleyball hard. Her friend Kira, who was on the other side of the net, dove to reach it. Then Mallory rotated through other training exercises. She did crunches and jump squats. Kira lifted dumbbells. Then the girls switched exercises. Mallory and Kira were practicing for tryouts in a few weeks.

"I'll grab the ball for us after I get a drink," Mallory told Kira.

"Can you grab my water bottle too?" Kira asked. "I'm going to the bathroom."

"Sure."

Mallory and Kira met on the volleyball team when they started high school. They became close right away because they loved telling jokes and making their other teammates laugh.

This year, both girls felt sure they would make the team because they were returning players. But making the team wasn't their only goal. They both wanted to land a starting spot. However, there were only six starting spots, and everyone would be competing for them.

"Wouldn't it be fun if we both started this year?" Mallory said.

"Yes!" Kira said, with a smile. Then she served the ball over the net. It landed between two cones. "That's one!" she said.

TALK ABOUT IT

= In what ways might teammate relationships be the same as or different from other friendships?

= Have you ever been part of a sports team or club where you had to compete against friends? How did you feel leading up to the competition?

"Today, I want to place ten serves in a row by those cones. Serving accurately will give me a better chance in tryouts."

"Oh yeah," Mallory agreed, "I can only think of one other girl who can serve like you! And it's not me," she said with a laugh.

"Yeah, but your serves are so powerful—you don't need to be as accurate," Kira replied.

Mallory did a sprint workout while Kira continued to serve. She heard the ball smack the ground over and over. After a few reps from one end of the gym to the other, Mallory took a break before starting again. Kira paused too.

"Maybe I'll just stop at eight." Kira stopped and wiped her forehead. "I mean, that's better than I did yesterday."

"Kira, you can't quit!" Mallory stood up. "I know you can do ten. Let's go." She clapped her friend on the shoulder.

***

Finally, the day of tryouts arrived. Mallory and Kira felt confident with how they did, but they were still anxious to see the results. Mallory dried her hair after showering and thought about the coming season. The first game was a month away, and it was against the school's biggest rival. The next big game was

- **What are some benefits to having a talented teammate to compete against?**
- **What are some challenges of competing against a friend?**

homecoming week. She couldn't wait for that game because it always drew the largest crowd.

Later, Mallory and Kira quickly walked to the gym with a

few other potential teammates. Tryout postings were taped to the gym door.

"Yesss!" Kira said and pumped her fist. She had gotten a starting position, but Mallory hadn't. When she looked over at Mallory, Mallory tried to celebrate, but she had mixed emotions.

"Congrats, Kira! You did it!" Mallory said. She gave her friend a hug and a weak smile.

"Thanks, Mallory," Kira said. "I'm sorry you're not starting. You worked really hard."

"Yeah, and so did you," Mallory said. She was proud of her friend and knew Kira deserved to be a starting player. But she was still disappointed her name was lower on the list. She took a step back to let other people read. She imagined her first game, sitting on the bench watching Kira start. She really wished she would be starting with her. It might take a little while for her to get over the disappointment. But she knew that when that first game came, she would be cheering the loudest for Kira.

TALK ABOUT IT

- Why does Mallory have mixed emotions? What might she be feeling?

- How can teammates stay friends while competing against each other?

- What can you say or do for a friend who is disappointed they didn't reach a goal?

- Should you expect friends to celebrate with you no matter what? Why or why not?

ASK THE

EXPERT

When Kira got a starting position and Mallory didn't, Mallory was conflicted. She could have been jealous of or upset with Kira, but she remembered their friendship. She was happy for Kira and proud of her success.

Competing against friends can spark difficult emotions. You may be frustrated if you perform less than your best or are beaten. You might want revenge or get upset after an unfair play. During tryouts or a close game, you might wish for another girl to mess up so you can get ahead. All these emotions challenge how you act, but don't let them ruin your friendship. Praise others when they deserve it, and be honest if you're frustrated or don't want to talk about a certain game or practice. One way to handle competition stress in the moment is to focus on yourself instead of others. Take a deep breath and think positively. If an unfair call is made, remember that it's out of your control and let it go.

Even when teammates compete against each other, they can still be friends. Friends want what's best for each other. They don't want to see the other person fail. Most of all, knowing you have a supportive teammate on your side helps you feel confident and capable.

GET HEALTHY

- When you're stressed or frustrated, take a deep breath and remember to focus. Take a moment to clear your head and think positively.

- Think about a friend's feelings first. Don't rub a win in someone else's face. Try to cheer on teammates when they need a boost.

- Focus on being your best. A hardworking attitude is healthy and responsible, and it can easily rub off on others.

- Encourage others to be their best.

THE LAST WORD FROM EMMA

I learned a lot of lessons from being on the dance team in high school. Each girl on our team had a different personality. After a long day of practice, we often got annoyed or frustrated with each other. Sometimes my teammates harshly critiqued each other's performance. Judging someone can quickly lead to hurt feelings or a damaged friendship. On the other hand, pointing out what others did well and letting the negative things go encouraged us all to keep working hard. I learned that cheering on my teammates made practice positive and strengthened friendships on the team during challenging times.

CHAPTER NINE

OUTGROWING A FRIENDSHIP

How have your interests changed since you were young? Do you still play the same games or watch the same shows? What types of books do you read? How have your opinions about news, school rules, or other issues changed? Changes during adolescence are normal, but they can cause you to outgrow a friendship. Even though ending and starting friendships is natural, it is not always easy.

Seeing a friend hang out with other people may hurt your feelings. Being assigned to a separate class from your best friend can make school less fun. Extracurricular activities can take time away from friendships or lead to new friends.

For these reasons and more, you may feel certain friendships become distant. You might not talk to a friend for weeks, or when you finally meet up with a friend, the conversation is awkward. Suddenly, you don't have much to talk about.

Every friendship is unique, and there is no formula for how to deal with losing a friend to a club, different school, or new group of friends. However, you can take comfort knowing that outgrowing a friendship is a natural part of life. Friendships don't

> Friendships don't stay the same forever.

stay the same forever. You can watch for signs of social change and prepare yourself to let some friends go when the time is right. That's what Elle did after hiking with her friend Suran.

ELLE'S STORY

"Is Suran coming over to bake with you tonight?" Elle's mom asked while unpacking her work bag. She set some folders on the counter.

"I'm not sure," Elle said. "I texted her, but she hasn't replied yet."

"OK, just wondering. I love when you girls make something delicious," she said with a smile.

"Yeah, I'm going to look up a new recipe and do homework until Suran answers," Elle said, and she walked out of the room.

Elle opened her school laptop. She decided to check social media before starting her work. She looked at a few posts, and then Suran's name came on-screen. Elle got distracted looking through Suran's profile. She and Suran had been friends for

many years and had lots of fun memories together. But they hadn't seen each other very much lately. All of Suran's recent photos showed her with other girls from school. Elle wasn't upset, because she knew Suran had an outgoing personality and made lots of friends easily, but she did miss spending time with her friend.

TALK ABOUT IT

= Do you talk with a parent or trusted adult about your friends? Why or why not?

= What are some positive and negative ways social media can affect friendships?

= Elle misses her friend, but she's not angry at her. Have you ever been in a similar situation? How did you feel, and what did you do?

By the time Elle finished her homework, Suran still hadn't replied to her text. *I guess we won't be baking anything tonight,* Elle thought.

* * *

At school the next day, Elle saw Suran in the hallway. She went up to Suran's locker.

"Hey, Suran!"

"Oh, hi, Elle! Sorry I didn't text you back last night. Right after I saw your message, I had to take the dog on a walk, and then I forgot to respond."

"Oh, that's OK. I was able to get ahead on my homework, and I found a great new recipe for us to make!" Elle imagined the delicious-looking sweet potato pudding cake again. She knew Suran would love it. Sweet potatoes were her favorite.

"Nice!" Suran said, with a smile. "Well, I've gotta go to class. I'll see you later!" She turned and walked away.

Elle went the opposite direction, but she could hear Suran's laugh ring out behind her. Elle glanced back and saw Suran in a circle of girls at the end of the hallway. Elle felt her cheeks warm. It seemed like Suran rushed off to hang out with other girls instead of hurrying to class. Then Elle shook her head and continued walking. She didn't think Suran would purposely be rude like that.

TALK ABOUT IT

▪ **What can a girl do if her feelings get hurt by a friend?**

▪ **Have you ever been confused by a friend's actions? What happened? Did you ask the friend about the situation, or did you only think about it from your point of view? Why?**

▪ **How can a girl balance being friends with multiple groups of people?**

***

95

Despite multiple calls and texts, Elle and Suran didn't have a chance to hang out for more than two weeks. Elle made a different treat at her house one night but saved the sweet potato pudding cake recipe for Suran. Finally, the girls caught up at Elle's house after school one day.

> Elle and Suran didn't have a chance to hang out for more than two weeks.

"So, what should we do?" Elle asked. "We could bake something, like we usually do. I found a recipe with sweet potatoes that you would probably love! I tried to tell you about it in the hallway a few weeks ago, but you rushed off." Elle looked at Suran, hoping she would explain what happened.

"Yeah, sorry about that. I was on my way to class when I got stopped by some other girls. Anyway, I do love sweet potatoes," Suran said, smiling, "but I don't really feel like baking tonight. Do you want to go on a walk instead? Or I could drive us to a cool hiking spot I went to last weekend," Suran suggested. She looked excited.

"Uh, OK, I'll try it! I've never really hiked before," Elle said. "Let me just change into better clothes." She went upstairs to change,

and then Suran drove them to the hiking spot. They bobbed their
heads to the music during the short ride.

Crickets chirped in the grass around them, and sticks
snapped under their feet. The girls hiked together, but they
didn't talk very much. Suran walked fast because she knew the
trail route, so Elle focused on keeping up. While she walked,
Elle thought about how different she and Suran had become.

She still preferred baking, while Suran seemed to be more into outdoorsy things.

"Isn't the view awesome?" Suran asked when they reached a small peak.

"Yeah, it is," Elle agreed. The sun had almost set, and the sky burst with deep orange colors. They watched the sun go below the horizon and then hiked back to the car.

When they returned to her house, Elle gave her friend a hug and said goodbye.

"Thanks for bringing me on a hike tonight! It was fun to do something new together," Elle said. But deep down, she still wished they had baked. Some of Elle's favorite memories were of Suran and her listening to music in the warm kitchen while waiting for their creations to come out of the oven.

"Yeah, no problem," Suran said. She drove away, and Elle walked back inside. She was a little sad that her friendship with Suran seemed to be fading. But she decided she would try the new recipe tomorrow night anyway. She might just bake by herself. But maybe she could invite a different friend to join her if she felt up to it. Elle still enjoyed baking, and she knew it would be fun to make more baking memories with someone else.

TALK ABOUT IT

= How can you react when a friend wants to try something different?

= What are some signs that a friendship might be fading?

ASK THE

EXPERT

Elle and Suran had lots of great memories together, but they eventually grew apart. They didn't intentionally ignore each other or break up their friendship. Elle calmly thought about the situation rather than getting angry at Suran. She tried a new activity while still making time to do what she loved.

Unfortunately, not all friendships end well. Your friends may change, but that doesn't mean you have to. You should be yourself and do what you love. Don't let others push you to change. In fact, if friends become pushy or mean, those actions are signs that it's time for your friendship to end. A true friend wants you to be happy and wants what's best for you.

Friends are a wonderful part of life, but friendships don't always work out how we hope they will. Sometimes the plans you make with friends don't end up happening. As time goes on, you may find yourself growing closer to or farther from certain people. Take time to think through a friendship if you need to. Don't feel like you have to rush into any decisions about ending friendships. Be patient and respectful during times you drift apart or don't see each other. Keep an open mind in case you reconnect later. Let time show whether you have things in common with a new friend before jumping into a different friendship.

In the end, you can be friends with as many people as you want. You get to choose whom you spend time with and whom you trust with your thoughts and feelings, and other girls get to do the same.

GET HEALTHY

- Let friends know if plans change. Keeping friends aware of your schedule helps avoid confusion and hurt feelings.

- Watch for signs of an unhealthy friendship. If a friend treats you badly, doesn't listen to you, or tries to make you do dangerous activities, it is time to end the friendship.

- Continue to do activities you like, and be yourself. Sometimes friends naturally outgrow each other, and that's OK!

- Be honest and kind. Whether a friendship is beginning or ending, you should respect the other person.

THE LAST WORD FROM EMMA

I thought my first best friend would be my best friend forever. However, our lives changed in high school. We joined different sports teams and clubs. She met new friends quickly, and I hardly saw her. At first I was jealous of the other girls. I felt like they took my best friend from me. It wasn't until I became busy with my own activities that I realized what happened. We drifted apart because we had new interests and obligations, not because we didn't like each other.

When we saw each other in the hallway, we often waved, smiled, or stopped to chat for a few minutes. Those times reminded me of our sweet friendship. And when we both moved on and spent time with new friends, it was natural, not sad.

A SECOND
LOOK

Throughout this book, we followed a girl who got over a fight, another who learned how to meet new people, a girl who was friends with her sister, a girl who discovered that learning about other cultures can make friendship stronger, and more. The stories showed different friends dealing with the ups and downs of life.

You may have related to some of these stories. At times, they may have been a little challenging. Perhaps it is because when it comes to friendship, we don't have a formula. Supporting others, forgiving friends, and navigating adolescence looks different for everyone. You may have to balance friends with school, clubs, sports, your family, or your neighborhood. The friends you like most might live far away or be super busy and hard to spend time with.

Most kids know that having friends is healthy for their social lives. But knowing how many friendships to try to balance may not be so straightforward. Rely on your instincts and on what feels right for you. Yet even if you stay absolutely true to yourself, you may still find yourself in a difficult position, such as on a competitive sports team, at a new school, or in a fight. It's natural to feel alone at times because your life journey is unique to everyone else's. During adolescence, you and your friends will develop your own identities. Remember to give yourself space to explore friendship in positive ways.

Don't beat yourself up for making a mistake or putting yourself out there to meet new people. Learn from your choices, and pay close attention to your own reactions. Grow as an individual and as a friend, and that will help you find people who will support you during all times of life.

XOXO,
EMMA

PAY IT FORWARD

Healthy friendships are all about staying true to yourself, giving and receiving support, and having fun! Discovering ways to build friendships is a journey that changes throughout your life. Now that you know what to focus on, you can pay it forward to a friend too. Remember the Get Healthy tips throughout this book, then take these steps to get healthy and get going.

1. Seek out and celebrate friends who have different backgrounds from you. Friendship can break down cultural barriers if you're willing to learn, grow, and support the uniqueness of others.

2. Be yourself, and you'll find friends who share your interests. Don't pretend to be someone you're not. Let friendships grow naturally.

3. Remember that everyone makes mistakes. Friends can recover from a fight by listening to each other, making sincere apologies, and forgiving each other.

4. Think of ways you can introduce yourself or start a conversation with someone new.

5. Stay loyal to friends. Two key parts of true friendship are being trustworthy and respectful. Only share a secret if someone could be harmed if you remain silent.

6. Let your social circle have a range of friendships. Having best friends, acquaintances, and friends in between is a healthy balance of many relationships.

7. Be open to growth. Teammates can work hard together and improve their skills, or friends can explore together and try new experiences.

8. Ask a parent or other trusted adult to share about a friendship that ended. See what you can learn from his or her story.

9. Keep a personal journal to reflect on your feelings and the changes in your life.

10. Reach out for help in hard times or show you care when a friend is struggling.

GLOSSARY

compromise
To settle differences by a partial yielding on both sides.

confide
To share a secret with someone having great trust and confidence that he or she will protect the secret.

cope
To deal with a personal issue or overcome a difficulty.

critique
To give feedback for improvement.

dignity
Conduct that is respectful.

diverse
Different from one another.

empathy
Being able to understand and share another person's thoughts and feelings.

extracurricular

Relating to student activities, such as sports, that are connected with school but that do not carry academic credit.

intimate

Very familiar with or close to another person.

obligations

Responsibilities a person must fulfill.

process

To handle a situation emotionally, mentally, and physically by careful thought and action.

ADDITIONAL
RESOURCES

SELECTED BIBLIOGRAPHY

"Healthy Friendships in Adolescence." *US Department of Health & Human Services*, 25 Mar. 2019, hhs.gov.

Heid, Markham. "How Many Friends Do I Need?" *Time*, 18 Mar. 2015, time.com.

Partridge, Julie. "The Role of Friendships in Youth Sports." *NAYS*, 11 Feb. 2015, nays.org.

FURTHER READINGS

Harris, Duchess. *Growing Up LGBTQ*. Abdo, 2020.

Hemmen, Lucie. *The Teen Girl's Survival Guide*. Instant Help, 2015.

Whalen, Lauren Emily. *Dealing with Drama*. Abdo, 2021.

ONLINE RESOURCES

Booklinks
NONFICTION NETWORK
FREE! ONLINE NONFICTION RESOURCES

To learn more about healthy friendships, please visit **abdobooklinks.com** or scan this QR code. These links are routinely monitored and updated to provide the most current information available.

For more information on this subject, contact or visit the following organizations:

Girl Scout Central

420 Fifth Ave.
New York City, NY 10018
girlscouts.org

The Girl Scouts of America support girls as they grow, make new friends, and learn new skills.

GirlsHealth.gov

Office on Women's Health
U.S. Department of Health and Human Services
200 Independence Ave. SW, Room 712E
Washington, DC 20201
girlshealth.gov
800-994-9662

GirlsHealth.gov is run by the Office of Women's Health. It provides health information to women and girls on topics such as feelings, relationships, and bullying.

I Am B.E.A.U.T.I.F.U.L.

4850 Golden Pkwy., Suite B230
Buford, GA 30518
iambeautiful.org
404-545-9051

This educational enrichment nonprofit builds self-esteem and leadership capability in women and girls of all ages. Programs support achievement of success in every aspect of life, including physical, mental, and spiritual.

INDEX

ABOUT THE
AUTHOR

EMMA HUDDLESTON

Emma Huddleston lives in Minnesota with her husband. She enjoys reading, writing, and swing dancing. She has two sisters and three brothers, and she is an aunt! She hopes this book helps girls navigate the fun, challenging, and rewarding world of friendship as they grow up.